SET PUZZLES

Find sets ▪ group them ▪ fill the grid

DAVE PHILLIPS

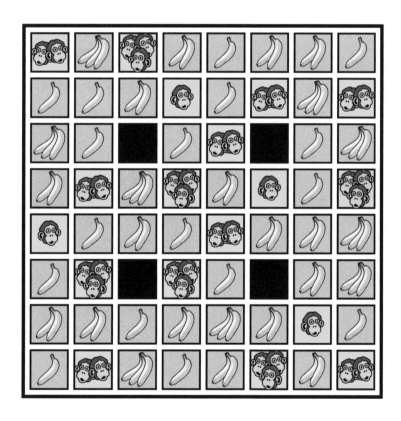

DOVER PUBLICATIONS, INC.
MINEOLA, NEW YORK

INTRODUCTION

The challenge of this unique collection is to organize each puzzle into "sets". A set is defined as a grouping of adjacent tiles that meet the conditions set forth for each puzzle. You are required to draw along the white channels between the tiles so that a set is surrounded and isolated from other tiles. When all tiles are grouped into sets according to the rules, the puzzle is solved. The black tiles are not included in any set. All puzzles in this collection follow these rules though the conditions required for each set differ greatly.

The difficulty of the puzzles increases in the order presented so you will acquire strategies along the way to help you solve the more challenging puzzles. You will find that you are able to form sets easily when tackling the puzzles initially, only to be thwarted by the last remaining tiles.

A useful strategy is to find adjacent tiles that cannot be included in the same set. By so doing, you can draw part of the wall separating sets. This may then provide a clue to find other wall sections. Another strategy is to discover "paths" from one tile to another that must share the same set; by so doing the tiles between must also be included in the set.

I have included a clue to help you get started in each of the 18 set categories. If you welcome these clues, it is best to tackle the challenges in order. The clue usually refers to the first puzzle in the upper left corner of the left side page. If I have done my job credibly, you will occasionally visit the back of the book to find a solution that you are convinced cannot possibly exist.

Have fun,
Dave Phillips

Dave Phillips is a full-time puzzle maze designer providing content for books and publications throughout the world. He also designs people-size mazes and games, including dozens of maize mazes each year. Visit his website at: *www.DavePhillipsPuzzleMaze.com.*

Bibliographical Note
Set Puzzles: Find sets, group them, fill the grid is a new work, first published by Dover Publications, Inc., in 2012.

International Standard Book Number
ISBN-13: 978-0-486-49055-7
ISBN-10: 0-486-49055-6

Manufactured in the United States by Courier Corporation
49055601
www.doverpublications.com

SET PUZZLES

Three Charms

Set: One of each charm.

Clue: Here is a nice easy first level. Since a set requires one of each charm, and there are three kinds of charms, each set must contain three charms. In the first puzzle, note the heart in the upper left corner, it must be enclosed with a star to make a set. If you imagine a path to a star that does not require grouping more than three tiles, you easily see that the star top center is the only possibility. When you include the moon between the two charms, you made your first correct set.

3

Four Charms

Set: One of each charm.

Clue: In this next level, an extra charm is added to the mix so a set consists of four charms. Note the star in the upper left corner of the first puzzle; there are two possible sets that could include it, though only one is correct. Not a good place to start. Note the green clover in the lower right corner, there is only one star that could accompany it, though two ways to get to it. One way forces a set to have two hearts so the other way must be correct.

Five Charms

Set: One of each charm.

Clue: Now we are up to five charms and bigger sets. So a good strategy is to think more about paths leading from one charm to another that has the least number of possible alternatives, preferably just one. With five charms in a set, though, it is difficult to find. Consider the star lower left of the first puzzle, how many moons can it reach? That gives you the other three charms for the first set and you know it must be correct.

Six Charms

Set: One of each charm.

Clue: Six charms now; though there are fewer sets to find (only four in the small puzzles), the paths over charms are more convoluted. In the first puzzle the flower upper left must reach a star and there are only four. Try tracing an invisible path to each without encountering more than one type of charm and without trapping other charms. The path takes two turns to the only possibility. After that the other sets almost make themselves.

Lottery

Set: One of each number, 0 through 9.

Clue: It may seem a little daunting at first since here a set requires ten numbered balls. However, in the small puzzles at least, there are only two sets to find. Assuming you mastered the last challenge of six sets, you know to look for paths from one number to another where there is only one possibility. In the first puzzle, the upper 7 cannot get to the lower 1 without hitting more than one of the same number or isolating numbers. There is only one other option.

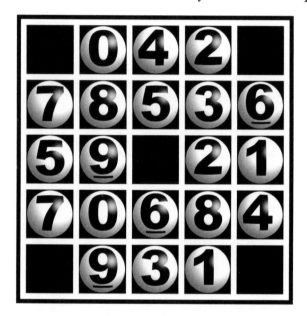

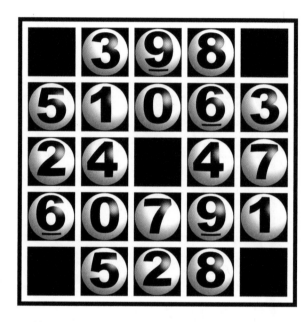

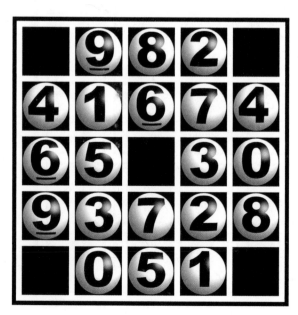

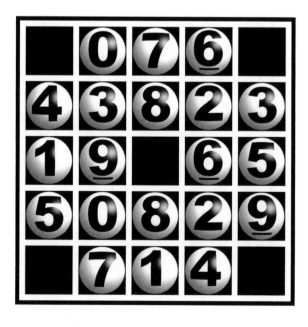

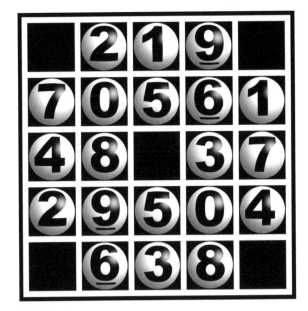

Color or Kind 1

Set: Three tiles that contain all the same color but different shapes, or all the same shape but different colors.

Clue: The tiles in these puzzles have two factors to consider not just one, as with the previous puzzles. You can choose to group tiles by color, in which case the shapes must be different, or you can choose to group tiles by shape, in which case the colors must be different. Both kinds may be included in the same puzzle. There is an easy way to get started, however; if two adjacent tiles have neither color nor shape in common, they cannot be grouped in the same set.

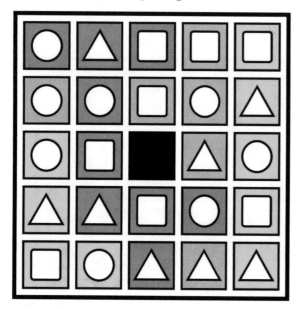

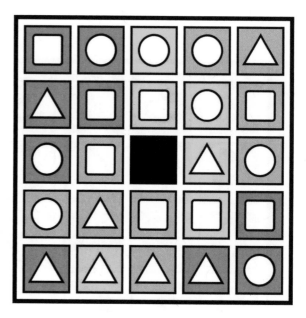

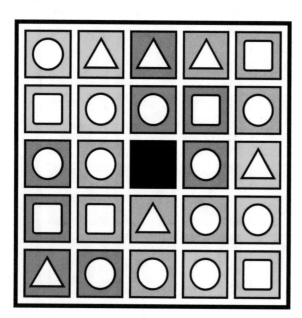

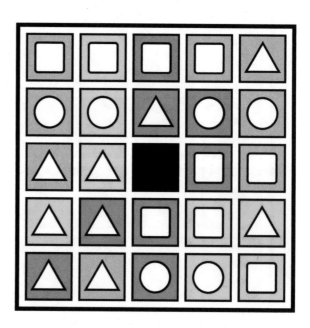

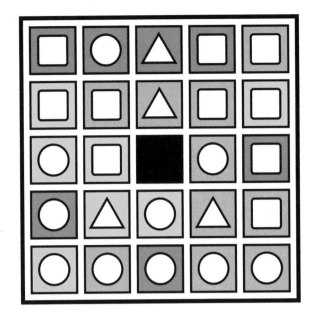

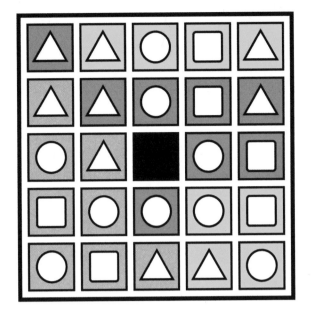

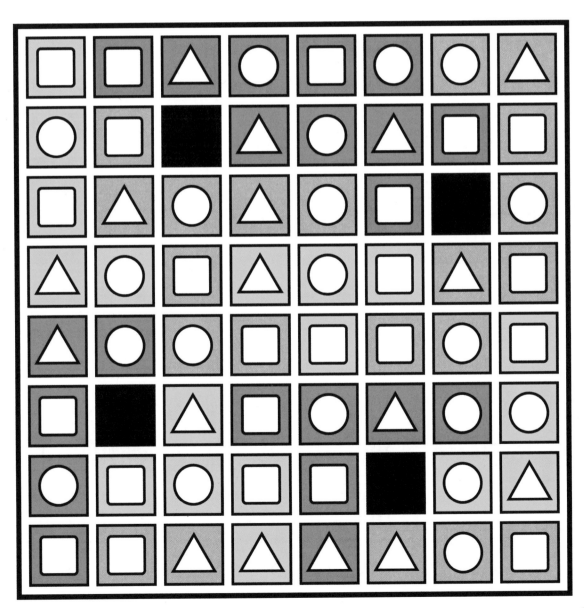

13

Color or Kind 2

Set: Three tiles that contain all the same color but different shapes, or all the same shape but different colors.

Clue: The number of tiles per set stays the same as the previous puzzles, but an additional color and an additional shape is added. After drawing a line between tiles that do not match color or shape, in the first puzzle, you will notice that the upper right tile must join with the one below it. There are two ways to go from there, however, and it is difficult to eliminate one of them. Look to expand other walls between tiles.

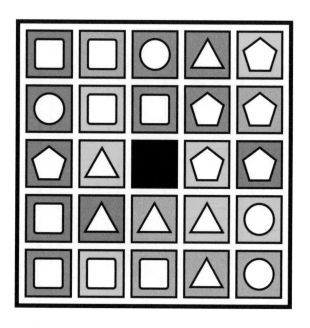

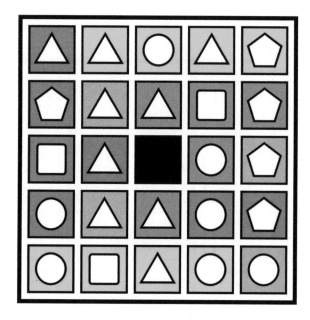

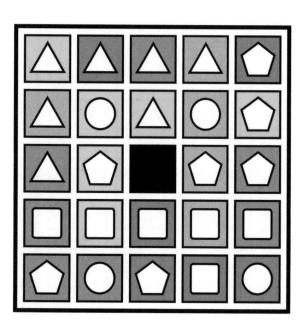

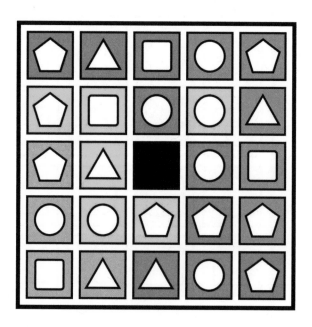

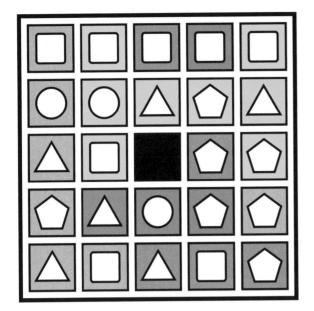

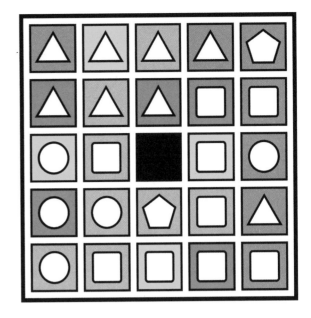

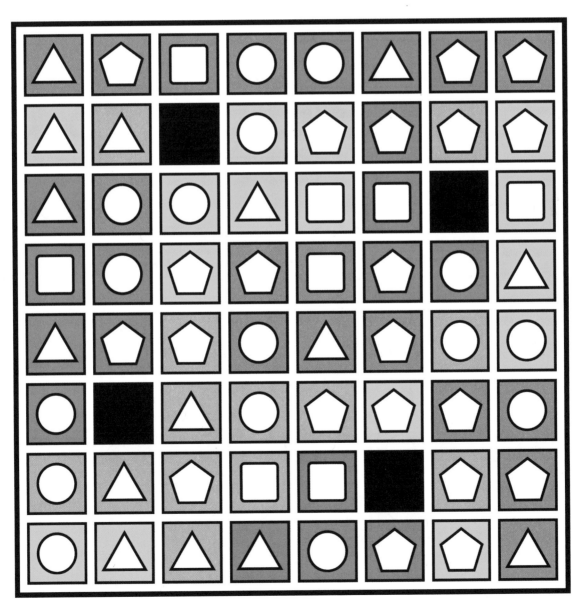

Color or Kind 3

Set: Three tiles that contain all the same color but different shapes, or all the same shape but different colors.

Clue: There are now five colors and five shapes to consider. In the first puzzle, after you find the wall sections as detailed in the previous two challenges, no clear set can be determined immediately. Consider the two right center triangles. If they were connected, the third tile would need to be another triangle with a different color. There aren't any available so you have discovered another wall section.

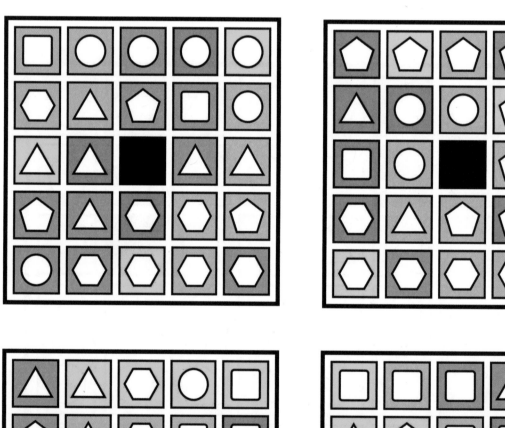

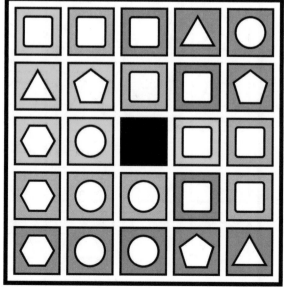

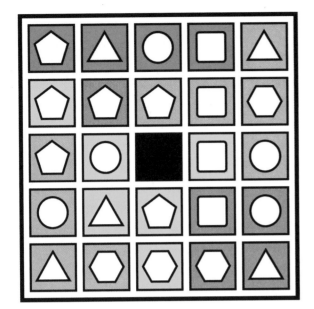

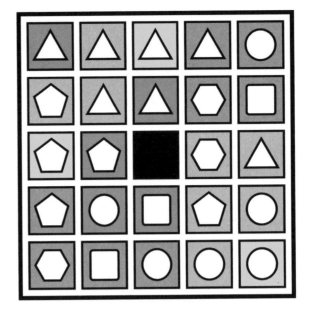

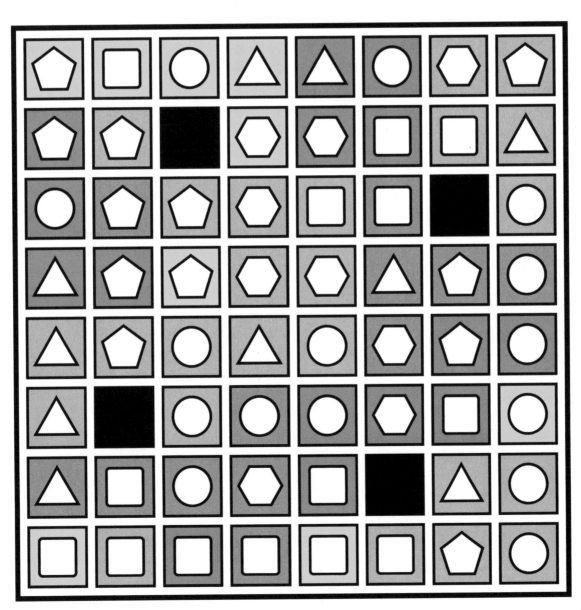

Two Pairs

Set: Four tiles containing one pair of each color sock.

Clue: There are no wall sections to fill in with this challenge. Each set must contain four socks: two white and two black. In the first puzzle, consider the black sock lower right. If it did not match with the black sock to the left, it would have to join with the black sock directly above, passing through two white socks. That would be okay if it did not create a set, far right, with four white socks.

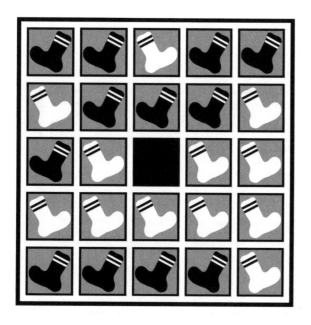

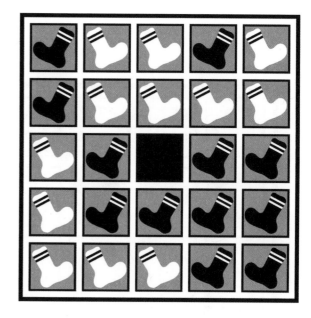

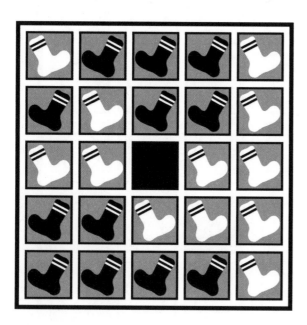

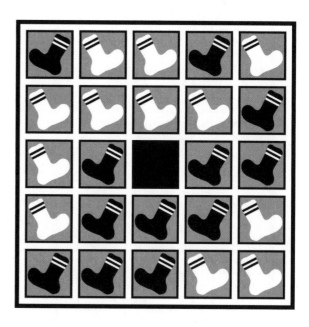

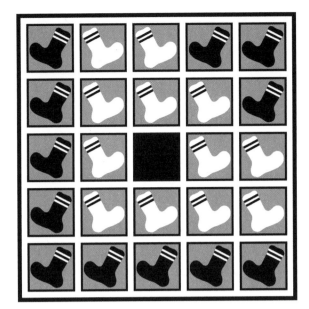

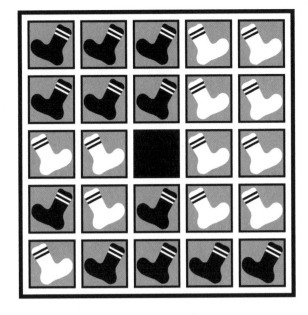

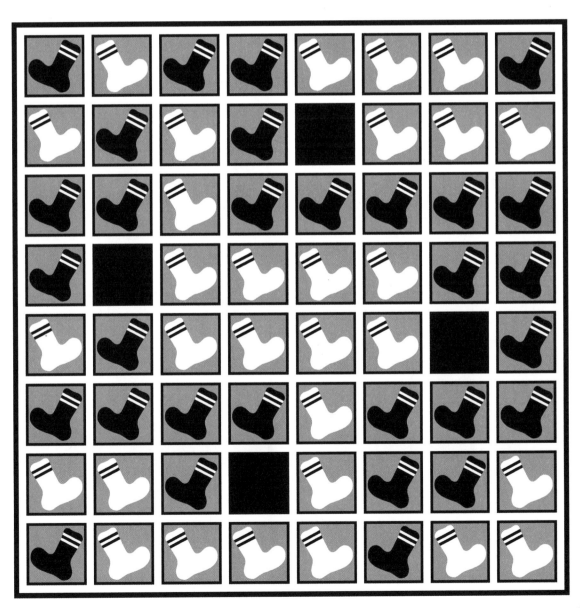

Three Pairs

Set: Six tiles containing one pair of three different color socks.

Clue: Two more color socks are added to the mix making it more difficult not to end up with odd socks. Since each set must contain three different pairs, one color pair is excluded from each set. In the first puzzle, there is no way for the yellow sock upper right to be included in a set with a white pair of socks.

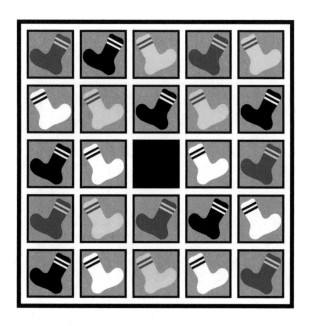

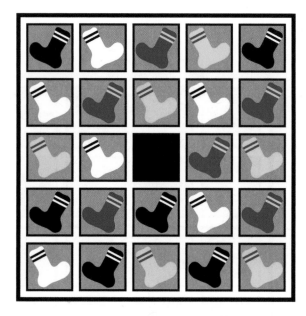

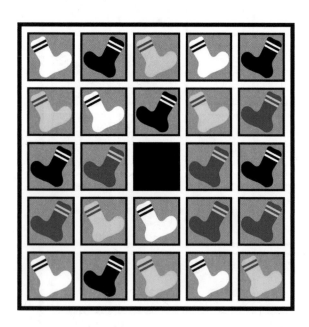

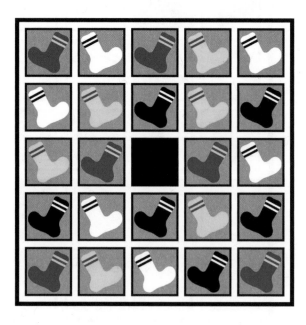

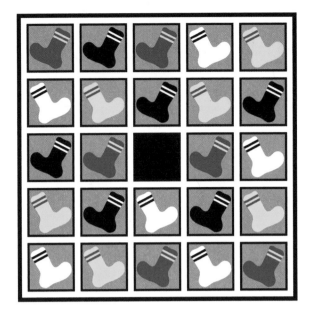

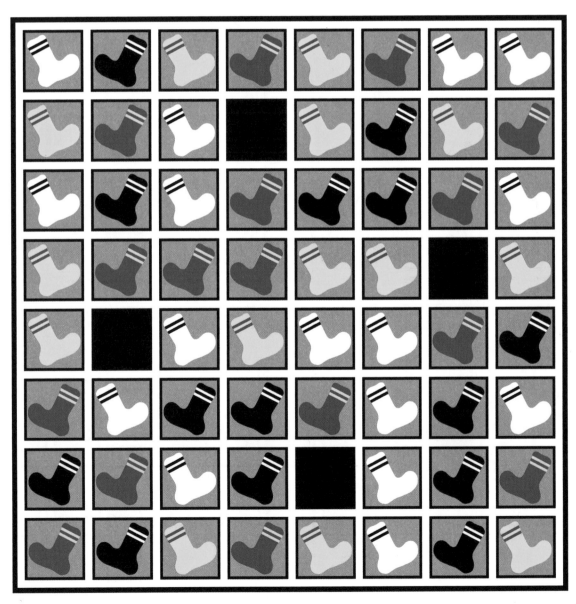

Nine

Set: Any number of tiles containing dice with a total of nine.

Clue: For the first time, the number of tiles in a set is variable. A set can be only two tiles or even as many as five. In the first puzzle consider the 6 in the bottom row. If it connected to the 1 about it the total count is 7, but the only option to get to the nine tally is the 2 to the left, leaving the 1 in the corner isolated.

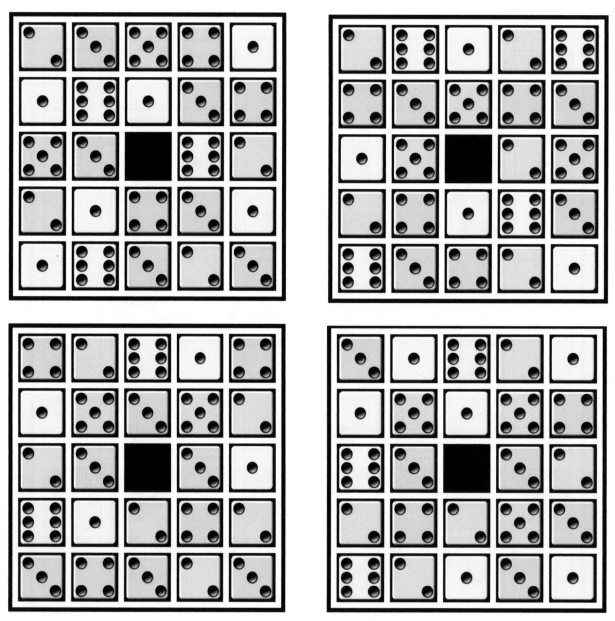

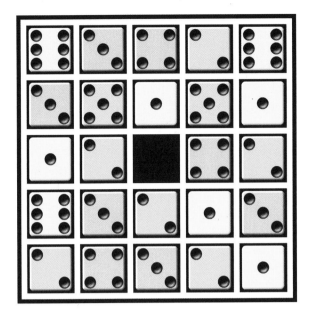

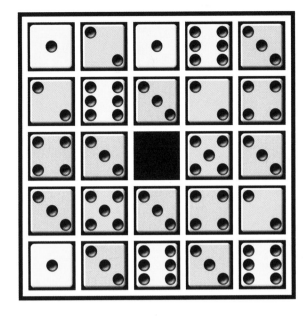

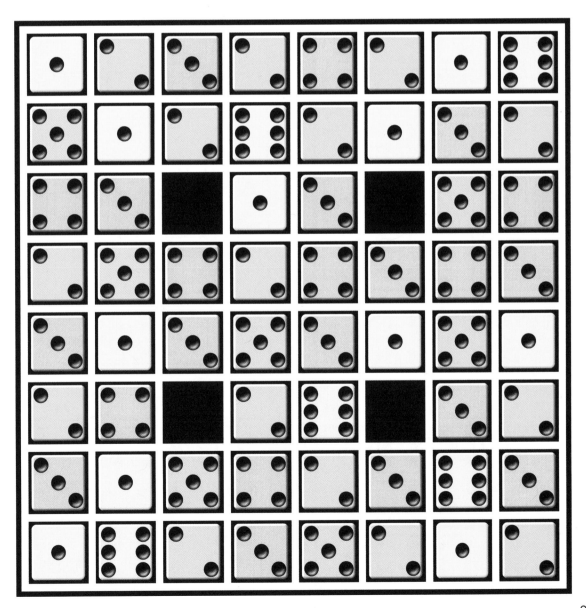

Seven or Eleven

Set: Any number of tiles containing dice with a total of seven or eleven.

Clue: In this challenge, either a total of seven or eleven is allowed which means more choices to lead you astray. In the first puzzle, consider the 3 lower right; if it is joined with the 1 above it, only two combinations equaling eleven is possible, leaving the 4, center right, without any possible way to get to seven or eleven.

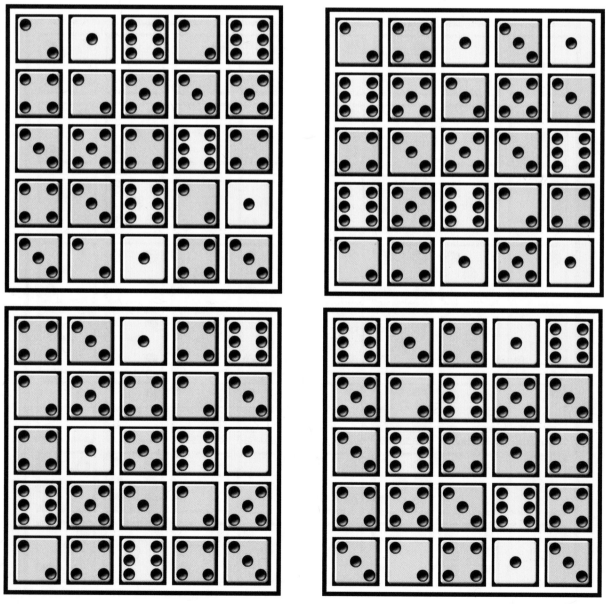

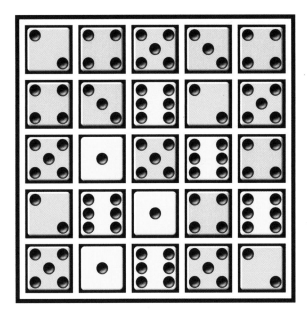

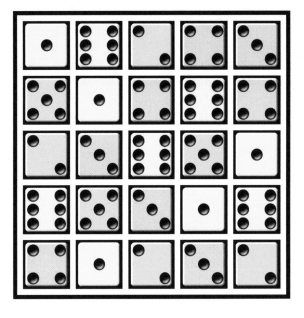

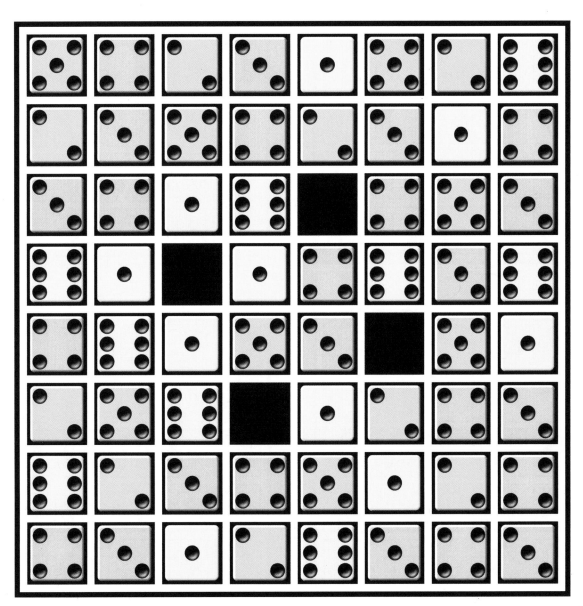

25

Two Pair or Better

Set: Five tiles that form a poker hand that has a value of two pair or better.

Clue: Poker rules apply here. Each set of five cards is required to form a poker hand of two pair or better. That includes three of a kind, four of a kind, full house (three of a kind and pair), straight (Ace may go before a 2 or after a King), flush (all same suit), or straight flush. In the first puzzle, consider the Ace of Hearts. It cannot be part of a flush or straight. There is no choice but to get to the Ace of Clubs, though there are three ways to do it.

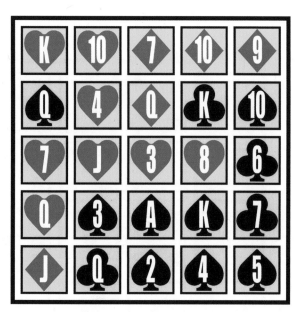

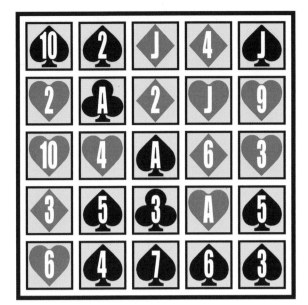

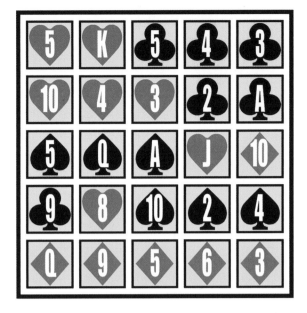

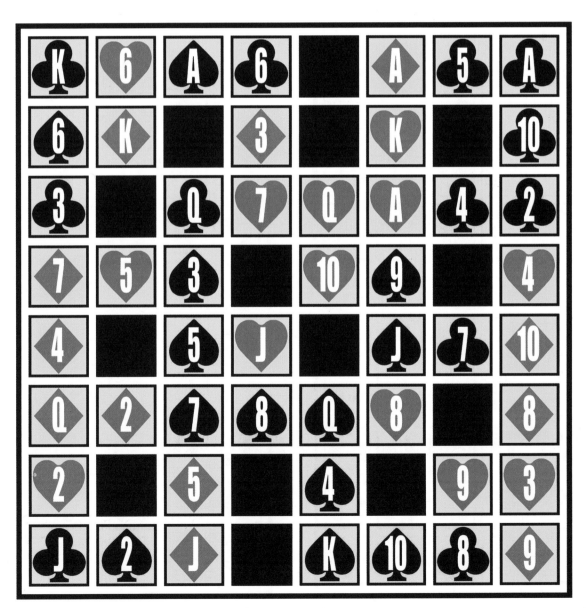

Jokers Wild

Set: Five tiles that form a poker hand that has a value of three of a kind or better. Jokers are wild which means they can be any card of your choice.

Clue: Poker is still the game, like the last challenge, only there is a Joker providing more choices and more confusion. This time two pair is not enough, however. Every card in the puzzle can find a path to the center Joker, adding to the challenge. In the first puzzle, consider the 10 of Clubs separated from the 5 of Spades. Find the options for the 10, and then see what is left for the 5.

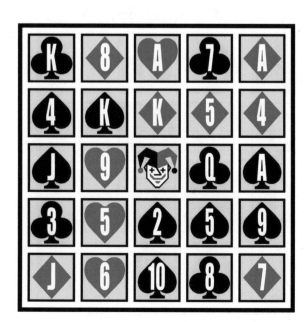

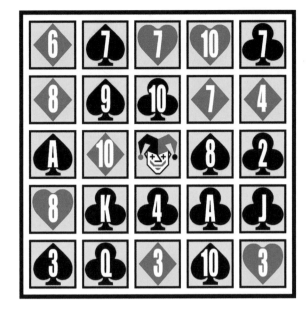

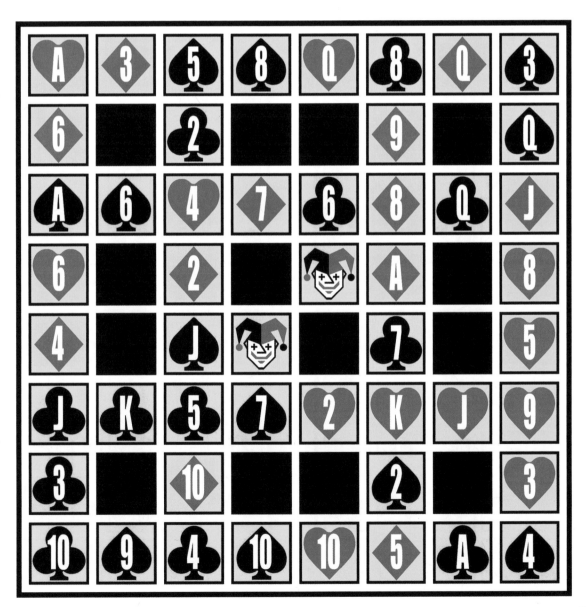

Set: Any number of tiles containing cards that total 21. Face cards count as 10; Aces can be 1 or 11; Jokers are wild which means they can be any card of your choice.

Clue: Jokers are still wild, Aces can be two values, and the number of cards is variable. At least all cards cannot find a path to the center this time. In the first puzzle, consider the Queen of Hearts. There is no way it can be separated from the Ace of Spades. The question is, however, does the Queen also connect with the King of Spades—is the Ace counted as one or eleven?

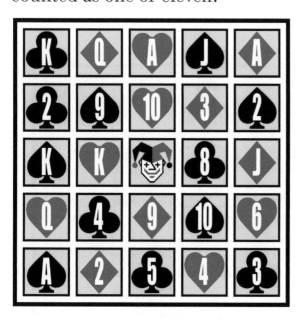

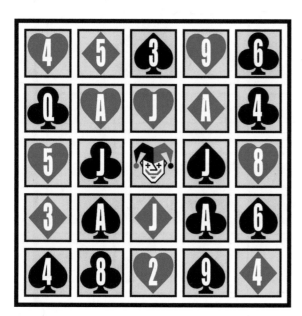

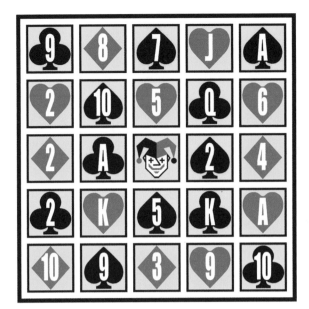

Monkeys and Bananas

Set: Any number of tiles that contain a single group of monkeys (one, two, or three) and enough bananas so that each monkey in a set has two.

Clue: This challenge may seem like a zoo at first, with so many demanding monkeys and bunches of bananas, but you should be quite skilled by now. While an easy wall section is one monkey adjacent three bananas it occurs only twice in the first puzzle and then once in the second puzzle. It is a better strategy to form paths from bananas to monkeys.

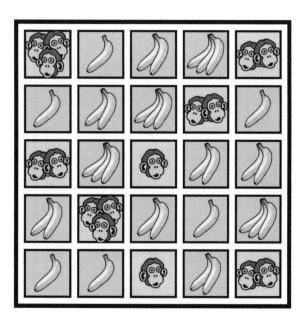

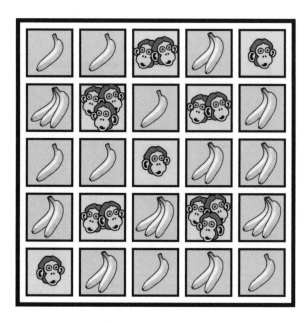

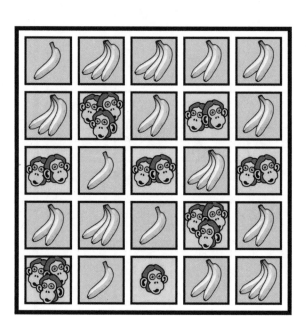

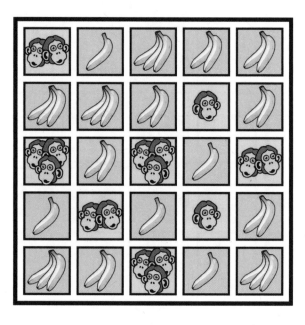

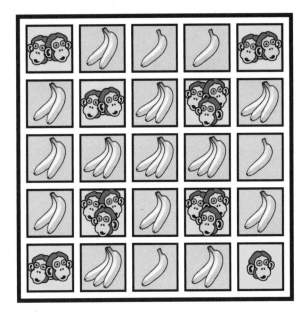

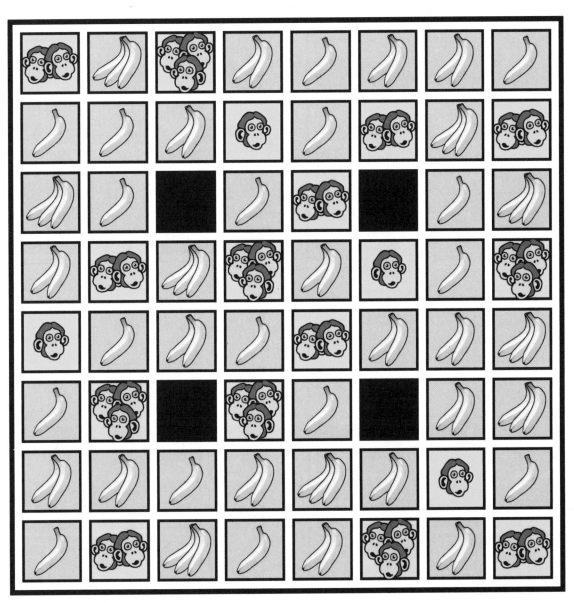

Squirrels and Acorns

Set: Any number of tiles that contain one squirrel and the same number of acorns as all the other sets.

Clue: This challenge is similar to the previous one though it is one squirrel at a time. Each squirrel needs the same number of acorns which changes from puzzle to puzzle. Naturally, you are smart enough to add the acorns, divide by the number of squirrels, to discover the number of acorns per squirrel. So you have the option of solving the puzzles without knowing the count, just in case the previous puzzles have been too easy for you. Though if they were, you would not be reading this.

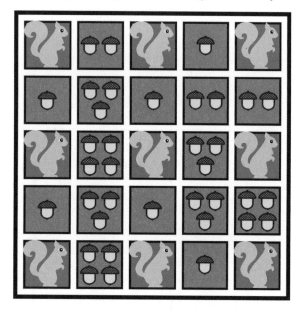

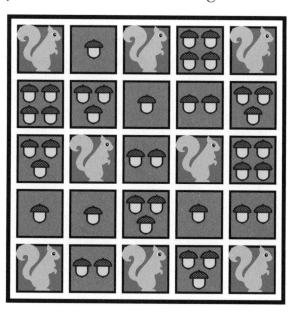

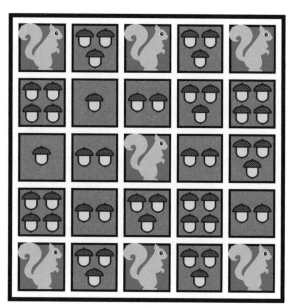

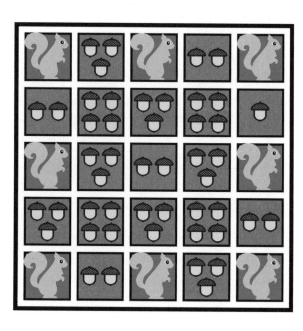

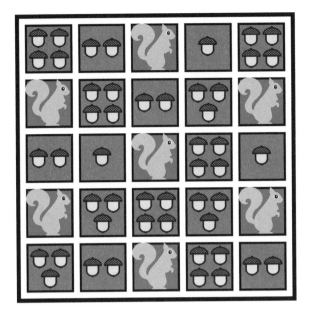

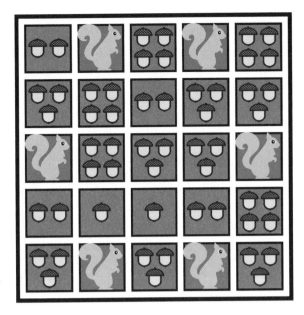

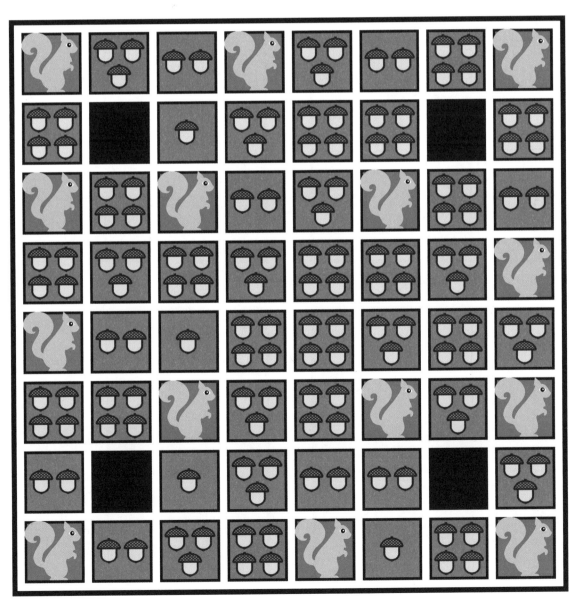

Spiders

Set: Contains a single spider but is the exact size and shape as all the other sets (can be turned any way and mirror imaged).

Clue: In this last challenge, all the sets in each of the puzzles must be the same shape and size, though you don't know what that shape is. It is easy to figure out the number of tiles per set, naturally, but the shape is the real trick since it can be turned and mirror imaged. A good strategy is to find all the possible shapes and try to eliminate ones that cannot work even before factoring in the spiders.

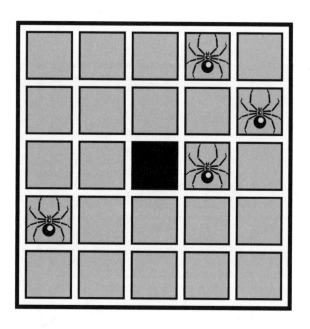

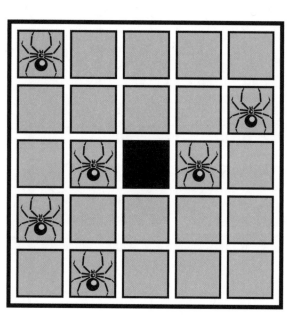

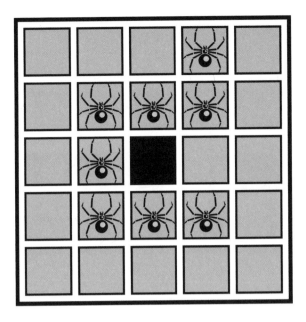

37

Solutions

Three Charms

page 2

page 3

Four Charms

page 4

  (page 5 grid)

page 5

Five Charms

page 6

page 7

Six Charms

page 8

page 9

39

Lottery

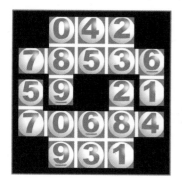   

page 10

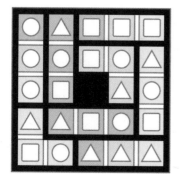 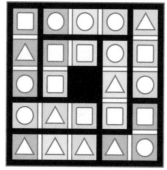 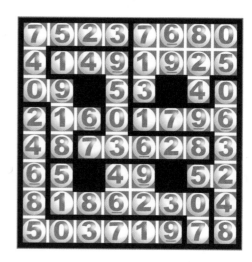

page 11

Color or Kind 1

  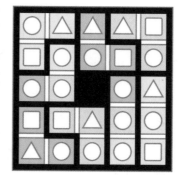 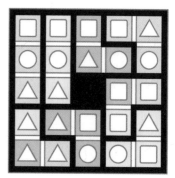

page 12

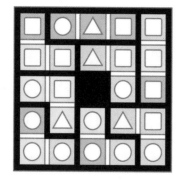 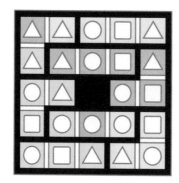

page 13

Color or Kind 2

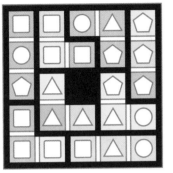 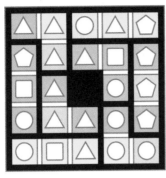 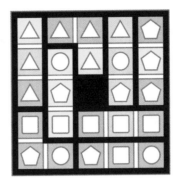 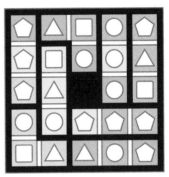

page 14

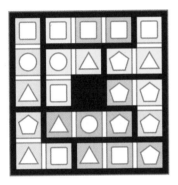 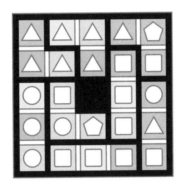 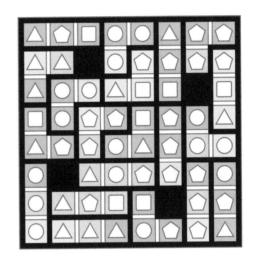

page 15

Color or Kind 3

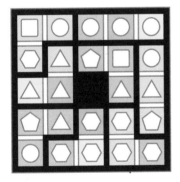 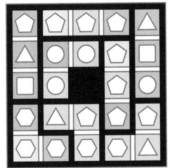 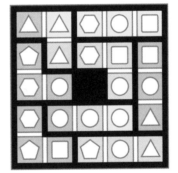 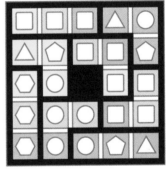

page 16

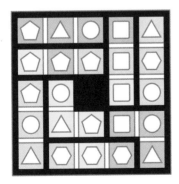 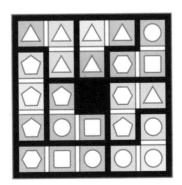

page 17

Two Pairs

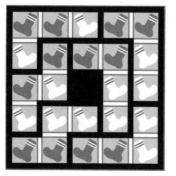 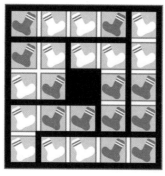 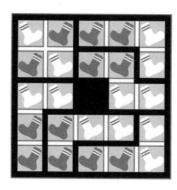 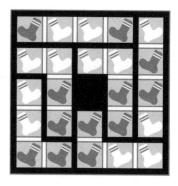

page 18

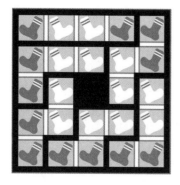 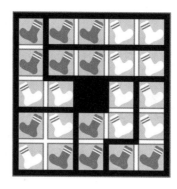 

page 19

Three Pairs

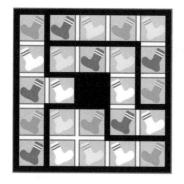  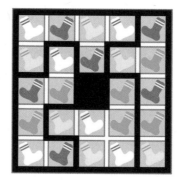 

page 20

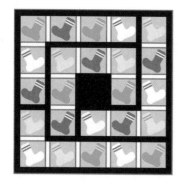 

page 21

Nine

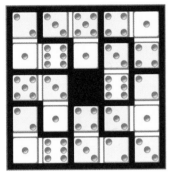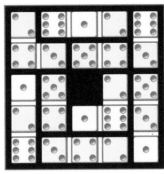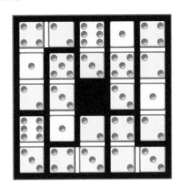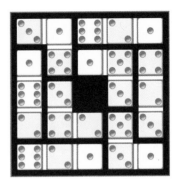

page 22

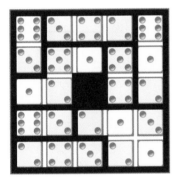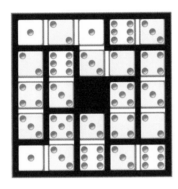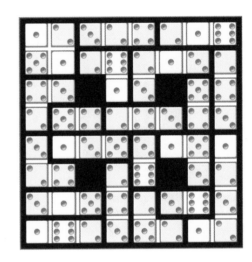

page 23

Seven or Eleven

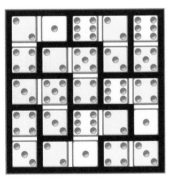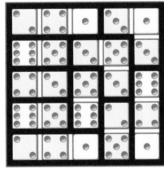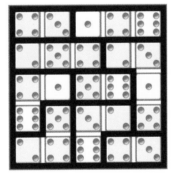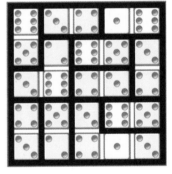

page 24

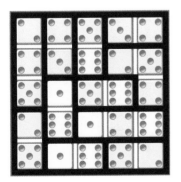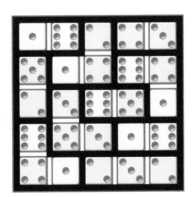

page 25

Two Pair or Better

page 26

page 27

Jokers Wild

page 28

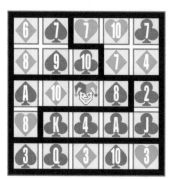

page 29

21

page 30

page 31

Monkeys and Bananas

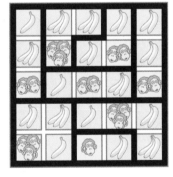

page 32

page 33

Squirrels and Acorns

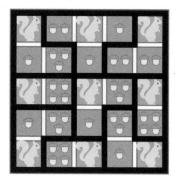 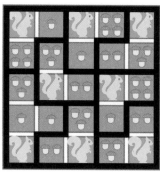 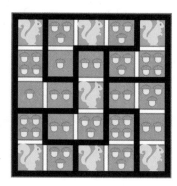 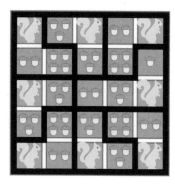

page 34

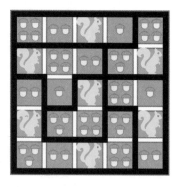 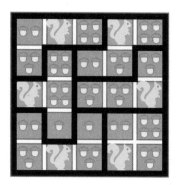 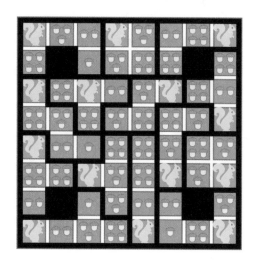

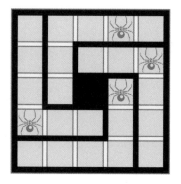  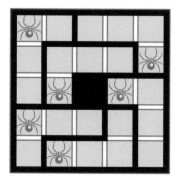

page 35

Spiders

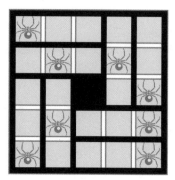

page 36

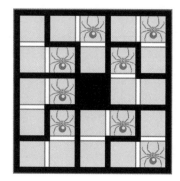 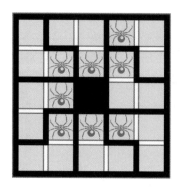

page 37